COPING WITH THE LOSS OF A DOG

HOW TO DEAL WITH THE DEATH OF YOUR FRIEND

RICHARD OLIVER

DEDICATION

This book is dedicated to Marley, my current companion, and the dogs I have lost; Pickles, Lincoln, Ben and Boris.

CONTENTS

CHAPTER 1

INTRODUCTION

Firstly, please allow me to extend my deepest sympathy to you for the loss of your friend, but please believe me when I say the feelings you are experiencing now will diminish over time and be replaced by happy memories.

That's not to say that you will never grieve for your pet years from now, of course you will, but those feelings will be a world of difference to the feelings you are currently experiencing.

I hope this book helps you navigate the rocky road ahead, which at the moment you no doubt can't see the end of.

It's written based on my experiences of pet loss and the heartache that followed, and I hope I can help you by explaining the process of grief and ways in which to make it more tolerable.

Before we begin our journey please allow me to introduce myself. My name is Richard and I have been a dog lover ever since I could walk and was able to stroke the family dog, Pickles.

I'm 42 as I write this book and have lost four dogs which I have grieved for, and still grieve for to this day.

Writing this is extremely hard as it brings back memories of every happy walk I ever shared with each of my dogs, and reminds me that one day I will lose the beautiful companion I now have.

Let me first explain that I am not a dog expert. I've never succeeded in training any one of my dogs to a level higher than what is expected of them, such as pooping outside and not biting people or dogs!

I am just a dog lover like you, who thinks he can help you with the journey that has led you to read this book.

Thank you for trusting me, and I hope I will be of some help to you.

Richard Oliver.

CHAPTER 2

WHAT IS GRIEF?

When we speak of grief we all have different ideas about it. Those of us who have experienced it will view it differently to those who haven't. To those lucky people it is still a concept. To us it is a reality.

The scientific description of grief suggests it is a natural response to the death of a significant person in someone's life. Of course animal lovers would argue that the death of an animal is just as relevant to them as the death of a person, and I fully agree.

I have lost people I loved and I have lost animals I loved, and although I didn't compare my grief between the two, the physical feelings and emotions I experienced were identical.

Love is love is love as far as I am concerned, and the grief a person feels after the death of an animal is just as real as for somebody who has lost a person, and never let anybody tell you any differently. To understand grief fully would be to understand love fully. Impossible.

We know deep down that both emotions are the response of chemicals released by our bodies, but that knowledge is useless when it comes to coping with powerful emotions that can even manifest themselves as physical symptoms.

. . .

The pain of grief is as real as the pain of a broken bone, and like a broken bone it takes more than a few days to heal.

But, and it's a big but for somebody experiencing the recent loss of a dog, the pain will become more bearable. Just like the pain of a broken bone will diminish over time, so will the pain of grief.

You may still get a small twinge of pain from a bone that's been broken years down the line, and the same is true for grief, but you must believe that it will become easier, even though at the moment nothing seems further from the truth.

If I were to sum up grief based on my experiences, I would describe it as a hole in the shape of the person or animal I had lost, right in the middle of my heart, and that hole needs time to heal, not filling with something that almost fits.

By that, I mean grief must be allowed to run its course or it will linger for longer than it is welcome or needed. Filling a dog shaped hole in your heart with another dog that doesn't quite fit isn't fair on yourself, or the dog you take on to try and replace the one you've lost.

In the next chapters I will try and guide you through the process of grief, and offer practical ideas that will help you to come to terms with the loss of your dog and cherish his or her memory.

I use the term 'He' to describe dogs in this book, as all my dogs have been male and it comes naturally to me to write that way.

CHAPTER 3

DEALING WITH GUILT

This chapter may not apply to everybody – not everybody feels guilt during grieving but many do.

The fact that you feel guilt shows that you cared about your dog. People who never cared for their dog during its life, certainly won't care about it after its death. That's not to say if you don't feel guilt you didn't care, everybody responds to grief differently.

Whether you were forced to have your dog euthanised, or he died of an accident or natural causes, you will probably be feeling some form of guilt about ways in which you perceive you let your dog down.

After the death of my second dog I struggled with guilt to the point that I blamed myself for his death, and nothing could have been further from the truth. It took me a while to realise it, but eventually I did.

People feel guilt for various reasons when a dog has died. It can be guilt from the idea you didn't exercise him enough or play with him enough, right through to the awful and unfounded guilt that you didn't spot the illness that took his life early enough.

When these feelings of guilt arise, you must take the time to notice each one and let it in. You have to acknowledge it before you can deal with it.

If you suddenly have the gut wrenching idea that your dog could have had a happier life, then really dissect that thought. Remember the happy times, of which there will be thousands. It's painful to draw on happy memories as much as it is to draw on sad ones when you're grieving, but you must.

The mind has a very clever way of only allowing certain thoughts through if you allow it to. I like to think of the mind as a vegetable draining colander, full of small round holes. The only thoughts that are going to get through that colander when you're grieving are the round ones – in this example bad thoughts.

You have to try hard to visualise all the good square thoughts that have been collected in the colander and turn them into round thoughts so they can flood through the holes and into your mind.

Let me try and explain that idea further.

My second dog died of cancer. He had to be euthanized. The vet told me that if the cancer had been discovered earlier he may have survived.

I wracked myself with painful feelings of guilt for weeks on end, hating myself for not spotting my dogs illness and getting him help earlier, and really taking myself to a place in my mind that I had never been before.

It was only when I spoke to a friend of my wife's, who happened to work in the mental health industry that things became easier for me.

She described the colander analogy that I have used and immediately pounced on the words the vet had chosen – '*If the cancer had been discovered earlier he may have survived.*'

As she pointed out to me, the vet had used the word *discovered*, not *spotted*.

It's a small difference but it made a huge change in my life. I spoke to my vet in detail and he explained that there was no way anyone could have '*spotted*' that my dog had cancer. There were no lumps or outward signs, and as soon as my dog began to go off his food I had taken him straight to the vet, and that was when the cancer was '*discovered.*'

Without a blood test or scan, which there would have been no reason to have done before my dog went off his food, there would have been no way to 'spot' the disease.

Just allowing this 'Square' thought through the colander helped me immeasurably and I realised that there was nothing I could have done to have prevented my dog becoming as ill as he did.

Your feelings of guilt, if you have them – not everybody grieves in the same way, will be different to mine, but I assure you that if you look for the square thoughts, the logical thoughts, they will be there. You have to let them in and you must believe them.

Your dog had a happy life, of course he did – you've chosen to read a book on how to cope with his loss. If you hadn't loved him and given him the best life you could, why would you be reading this?

Your dog knew that he or she was loved, and lived a happy and fulfilled life, and if you search for the thoughts that confirm that, they will be there – you just have to let them in. There is no place for guilt in your mind. Guilt is a damaging emotion unless it's founded, and for someone who loved their dog - it's not.

A quick exercise

When you find yourself becoming lost in thoughts of guilt about what you may, or may not, have done for your dog, try the following exercise.

Take a piece of paper and a pen and make two columns. Title the left column 'Good things' and the right column 'Bad things.'

Begin filling in the columns. Write all the good things you ever did for your dog in one column and things you think were bad in the right.

You will soon see that the good column far outweighs the bad column and if you really look at what's written in the bad column, nothing will be as terrible as you think it is.

You can even write an explanation next to any things you thought were bad, as to why they were done.

In my case, I once had to hit one of my dogs quite hard in the past, which was not something I ever did or do. I felt awful about it and it stayed with me, the guilt like a worm in my stomach.

When I discovered the two column exercise I wrote it in the bad column and concentrated on it. I'd hit Lincoln, my little Staffordshire terrier, and I felt awful. When I wrote the reason why I had hit him down, and really thought about it, I realised I hadn't had any choice.

I'd been walking him on a leash as we passed a field with a mare and her very friendly young foal. The foal was lovely and the mare let me pat and stroke it and hand feed it grass.

Suddenly, Lincoln – for reasons I never understood, leapt forward and dug his teeth into the foals mouth and nose. I hit him, not very hard but hard enough to make him release the foal.

Lincoln died a while back but I carried the guilt for hitting him for a long time. If I had just tried to concentrate on the rest of the walks we'd had together and the fact that I'd never laid a hand on him before or after, then my life would have been easier.

I should have also concentrated on the fact that Lincoln forgave me for hitting him.

Just think of all the times you've forgiven your dog – I bet there's loads! Your dog forgave you too. A dog – human relationship is a two way street, with forgiveness on both sides.

Your dog definitely wouldn't want you to be wallowing in guilt over things it had forgotten.

I still carry the guilt for the foal to this day though, but I made sure to check he was ok and came back the next day with an apple each for him and mum.

If I had never written that event down in my two columns I am certain that the guilt would still be with me today, overriding all the beautiful times Lincoln and I had together.

Just remember when you next feel guilty that there are far more memories that don't involve you feeling guilty, and let those memories in so you can enjoy them, just like your dog would want you to.

One last word on the subject of guilt.

Feeling guilty will never change anything. It will just strengthen the belief in your mind that you did something terrible. Let guilt go. Physically visualise it leaving you when it strikes and focus on non-guilty thoughts.

You deserve to be proud of the fantastic life you gave your friend, and your dog would certainly want you to be proud and happy.

CHAPTER 4

UNDERSTANDING OTHER PEOPLE'S REACTIONS

One of the hardest parts of losing a beloved dog can often be other people's reactions to your loss.

Unless you have a dog loving employer it's highly doubtful that you will be allowed any time off work, and work colleagues or even friends who don't own dogs will often take the attitude that it 'was just a dog.'

When the first dog I owned as an adult died, I was hurt at the reactions of friends and even some of my family.

Comments such as 'get another one to replace him' certainly weren't helpful – would they have said that if it were a human I'd lost? Of course not.

People who don't own or have never owned a dog simply don't understand the depth of love that exists between a human and dog.

I found there was no point in chastising people or taking offense. I just tried to understand their point of view and realised that they weren't intentionally trying to hurt me.

If you come across people like this, don't waste your time trying to explain your love for your friend and the grief you are feeling. It will only make things harder for you. Just forgive them and speak to somebody who does understand – there will be plenty of people out there who will understand and help you.

CHAPTER 5

LAYING YOUR DOG TO REST

One of the most emotionally draining parts of losing a dog is laying him to rest.

The process, by its very nature, is one that will leave you sad and overwhelmed. However, when your dog has been laid to rest in whichever way you choose, that's when the real healing can begin within you.

Laying your dog to rest is personal to you – never be swayed by what someone else tells you to do.

Personally, I have had my dogs cremated by my vet and received the ashes which I scattered around the areas I used to take my dogs.

I like to know that my dogs are still alive in the trees, leaves and flowers that I pass as I walk the same paths I used to with them. I love to imagine their spirits running through the trees as I pass, barking a silent hello.

The knowledge that your dog's ashes has nourished another life form can have a deep spiritual effect on you, whether you are religious or not.

Of course, you may feel differently and there are other options open to you.

Some people prefer to have their dog cremated and not receive the ashes. There is absolutely nothing wrong with this approach. You may not feel the need to have any part of the dogs physical remains – your memories may be enough for you.

There is of course the option of burial. Be aware that if you would like to lay your dog to rest on your property you should ask your local authority first, as some have strict rules against it.

Another reason to consider not burying your dog on your land is the fact that you may move home in the future, I don't think I would like to think my dog were buried at a property I was leaving behind.

Of course if you are renting a property this probably wouldn't be a good option.

Many people opt to have their pet buried at a pet cemetery. These cemeteries are mostly very well kept and of course you can always schedule a visit even if you ever move home.

The fact that the animal's grave has a headstone is of great comfort to many people.

The cost of a pet cemetery burial can be quite high and out of reach for some people, if you are one of those people try asking the cemetery owners about the cost of planting a tree there in memory of your friend – you could even sprinkle the ashes at the base of the tree if you choose cremation.

It's entirely your decision on how you lay your friend to rest, and in a later chapter I will go over other ways of permanently memorializing your dog, and provide some links at the back of the book to some interesting websites.

Planning the funeral or scattering of ashes

As mentioned above, the service will be an extremely emotional event for everybody who attends, especially children. (I cover how to speak to children in a later chapter.)

I have found over the years that the nicest way to say goodbye to your friend is to have the whole family present – don't keep the kids away if you have any, they need to say goodbye too. If you don't have any immediate family, bring a friend along, or even go alone if you so wish.

My family have always taken a walk along one of our dog's favourite routes and taken it in turns to scatter a few ashes in different spots. As we scatter the ashes we tell each other a funny story about the dog. Of course there are tears and it becomes very emotional, but we've always found it very therapeutic.

However you choose to lay your dog to rest try and include a portion of the service when you tell each other your fondest memories of your dog – it will help, I promise. It also helps cement those memories in your mind, rather than thinking about the sadness of the occasion.

Of course, there is never going to be an easy way to lay a dog to rest, and it's human nature to be upset, so each person must try and do what they think is best for them.

I can promise you though, that when the service is over and you arrive back home, the hardest part is over. It really is.

If you've chosen not to have a service and have left the ashes with the vet or pet crematorium, then there are plenty of ways you can have your service without physically laying your dog to rest.

I've read many accounts of people who simply walk the route they used to take with their dog, holding the dogs leash in their hand. Emotional, yes, but very symbolic and therapeutic. As hard as it is to accept, the sooner a human really realises that their dog has passed, the sooner they can heal their wounds.

You could simply spend time with the family printing off favourite photos of your dog and placing them in a photo album or frames. Tell each other stories about the dog as you do it, and reminisce as happily as you can.

I think it's extremely important that you take part in some form of ritual to recognise your dog's life otherwise people are prone to stay in a process of denial. This denial can manifest itself in awful ways and won't allow you to pass through the grieving process.

However you choose to remember your dog's life, make sure you say everything you want to say and focus on the happiest of memories. Your dog would have wanted nothing more from you.

CHAPTER 6

COMING TO TERMS WITH THE LOSS OF YOUR DOG

It's hard to believe you will ever come to terms with the loss of your dog but you will, eventually.

Coming to terms with the loss doesn't mean you will ever forget your dog, it just means that you will accept it has happened and you now need to move on with your life.

One of the biggest mistakes people make when losing any pet is immediately replacing it with another.

When you've lost a dog that had its own special personality and idiosyncrasies, another dog will never be able to fill his mould.

It's not fair on you and it won't be fair on the new dog. Only when you have come to terms with the loss of your dog should you even consider homing another.

This is all my opinion of course and I'm sure that many people would find comfort by immediately giving a new dog a home, but the majority of stories from people who have done it don't end well.

To come to terms with such an awful life event takes time, but there are ways to help yourself get there sooner.

One of the first and most painful things you should consider doing is removing your dog's belongings from sight at least. Even if you store them away in your garage or attic it's best not to be reminded that the bed is empty or the food bowl needs filling.

It truly is an awful thing to have to do and I feel callous writing it but it really should be done as soon as you feel able. If you can't bring yourself to do it, ask a friend or family member.

You will always have your photos and there is every reason to display them proudly, but photos are less of a physical reminder of the presence of your dog in the home.

You could even repurpose some of the dogs items if you wished. You could for instance grow a small plant in his food or water bowl and place it outside, somewhere prominent where you can always see it and remember him by.

Many people keep their dog's collar tucked away somewhere so they can reach for it in moments of real sadness and feel a connection with their pet.

The most important aspect of coming to terms with any loss is beginning to accept it, and unfortunately that does mean removing items from view that will continue to remind you of what you've lost.

You must allow your emotions free reign too - as long as the emotion is not unfounded guilt. You should cry as often as you like and laugh at happy memories just as often. Never feel like you are crying too much.

I have shed many tears over the loss of dogs and it did nothing but help me. Crying cleanses the soul and releases horrible balls of pent up emotion that will remain festering inside you if they're not freed.

Eventually you will find that as these emotions are freed, the time between them being released and replaced becomes longer and longer, until one day you will suddenly realise you are not thinking about your dog.

This can take time. I like to tell people that within six months most people have come to the point that they look back at their dog's life with fondness and tend to ignore the period of loss for the majority of the time.

What can you do to speed up this process? You could as my wife does, cry so many tears in a short period of time that you reach a point of acceptance a lot sooner, but each person is different and will grieve differently. I would suggest trying to concentrate on work, hobbies, entertainment – throw yourself into whatever way you have of passing your time.

Make sure you socialise as much as you can. Other people's conversation has the effect of taking your mind off your own problems. Meet up with friends and try not to talk about your loss, allow yourself to be dragged into what they want to talk about and you will find yourself becoming immersed in their world far more quickly than you could imagine.

Everybody and everything must die

It's an obvious statement but we don't really like to think about it too often.

Your dog *had* to pass away some day and unfortunately that day has been quite recent for you, and again I sincerely extend my sympathy.

Unfortunately for dog lovers, dogs don't have as long a lifespan as us. However, their lives are lived full of energy and full of fun and they don't give a diddly squat about the length of lifespans.

If we really try and accept that everything must die it becomes easier to accept the loss of a dog. It was inevitable, whether your dog passed away as a puppy in an accident, or as a senior dog in his sleep, it was always going to happen and there was never anything you as a caring owner could have done to prevent it – it was in the hands of God if you are religious or the hands of fate if you are not.

These thoughts are hard to process for most people, but to reach a point of acceptance they should be pondered now and again.

Acceptance comes to each person in his or her own way and timespan. Never feel like you are taking too long to grieve, you take as long as you need, but don't ignore the fact that you may be prolonging the process by not facing thoughts and memories that are uncomfortable.

Some people will purposefully try to block out happy memories because they are afraid of the emotions that will come hand in hand. These people will concentrate only on the sadness of their dog's death. I know this because it's precisely what I did when I lost Lincoln.

I suffer from bi-polar, and when I lost Lincoln I was going through a bad depressive period. I spent weeks not allowing myself to think happy thoughts about him and only concentrating on his death. I dug myself deeper and deeper into a hole until finally I allowed happy memories in – the colander analogy I used earlier.

I presumed that the way I had processed my thoughts was purely to do with my mental illness, but have since discovered that many people do exactly the same – they only focus on sad memories, as if to punish themselves.

If you can relate to this thought process then try spending ten minutes thinking of happy memories of your dog and happy memories alone. Make sure you smile or even laugh. Increase ten minutes to twenty minutes the next day and so on until your automatic reaction when you think of your dog is to smile.

It worked for me and I hope and believe it will work for you too.

Finally – never try and rush acceptance. Try and use some of the ideas I have written about, but if they don't work for you then you just need more time, and I assure you that you will reach a better place eventually. The human mind can only stay in a certain state for a limited period of time, and the state of sadness you are in will run its course in its own time.

CHAPTER 7

EXPLAINING THE LOSS OF A DOG TO CHILDREN

One of the hardest parts of losing a family dog is watching the reaction from children. I can still remember what it felt like as a child to lose a dog, but I can also remember that it didn't take me as long to come to terms with it as it does now I'm an adult.

Children, in my opinion, and from my experience should be treated in just the same way as an adult when it comes to the process of grieving for a dog. They should be given time and a little space and be included in all of the arrangements that follow the death.

My daughter was nine when she lost her first dog and she was devastated. She had lost other smaller pets previously such as Gerbils and goldfish, but never an animal that truly was 'part of the family.'

The approach I took was to allow her to cry and be angry, and I answered all her questions as truthfully as I could.

There is really not much more a parent can do for a child in grief except explain what has happened and that the dog is in a better place.

I've never lost a dog to an accident, but if I had, I think that unless my daughter had been present, I would have told her the dog had died of natural causes.

I don't think explaining the circumstances of an accident would help a child. I think telling small white lies in these circumstances is acceptable.

Children are far more resilient than we adults give them credit for and can often bounce back from a shock far more quickly than you could ever imagine.

Your child will obviously be devastated by the loss, but with a young age comes the ability to believe beautiful things.

My wife and I explained to our daughter that our dog had crossed a magical bridge and was now in a special place where dogs went when they had finished their lives.

We told her that her friend would be running around beautiful fields with hundreds of other dogs that were all friendly towards each other, and that he would look down on our daughter and make sure she was safe.

My daughter never questioned our story and she even became happy for our dog eventually. Happy that her pal was happy. It doesn't take a lot to please a child.

We included our daughter in the scattering of ashes, explaining that we were only scattering the body our dog had had to leave behind to be allowed to cross the magical bridge. We explained that the bridge is made of clouds and his body weight wouldn't have allowed him to cross.

My daughter is now twenty one and pregnant. Her due date is in December of this year. (2015)

She doesn't have a dog at the moment, but wants to get one as soon as the baby is old enough. She still talks about the magical bridge and how it meant so much to her to be given that happy idea. I have no doubt that when her child loses his or her first dog, it too will be crossing the bridge and joining the other dogs we've all lost.

One more thing to bear in mind is that a child can put a lot of pressure on an adult to get another dog quite soon after the loss.

My daughter was talking about another puppy within weeks of losing our dog. It is hard to refuse, especially when the child was so close to the pet, but it wouldn't be fair on yourself or a new dog to get one, after all its you that's going to have to do all the exercising and cleaning up after accidents.

You may find it too much to cope with having to walk a new dog that you weren't ready for in the same places you used to walk the dog you've recently lost.

My wife and I explained to our daughter that we couldn't start thinking about getting another dog until flowers appeared again on one of the bushes we had scattered some ashes nearby. We told her that it would be a signal from Ben that he was ready to allow another dog into his home.

We knew that flowers wouldn't start appearing for at least four months, and by the time they did she had stopped asking us anyway.

Every parent knows their child and will deal with the situation differently, but I would urge you to involve them in some sort of memorial service such as ash scattering or burial, it will help the child understand death and help them accept their pet has gone.

It's also a great idea to frame a photo of the dog and put it in your child's bedroom. I know my daughter appreciated it, and I did it because my mum did it for me when I lost my first dog as a child.

I can still remember holding that picture against my chest when I missed my dog.

I hope that what I've written has been of some help to you. Parenting is a very personal thing and you may come up with much more imaginative methods to help your child than I did.

However *you* deal with helping your child grieve, I hope he or she gets over the loss as quickly as possible.

CHAPTER 8

MEMORIALISING YOUR DOG

It can be highly therapeutic to memorialise your dog in some form. Some people do this by simply framing a small photo and other people get a tattoo of their dog with the animals ashes mixed in with the ink.

However you choose to remember your dog is personal to you but I've added this chapter to give you a few ideas you may not have thought of or heard of before.

I've never chosen to memorialise any of my dogs in any other way than photos or videos, so I can't speak from experience when I talk about these different options, but I have got a close friend who had a painting commissioned in oil of one of his dogs and it's something I may look into in the future.

I'll begin with the method I've used – photos and videos.

I was always click happy with a camera and when I got my first mobile phone with a camera I became far more click happy!

I literally have hundreds of photos of my dogs which at first I only saved on my phone and on social media sites.

I learnt a very valuable lesson early on when it came to saving photos on a phone and nowhere else. I lost over a hundred photos of my family, and the dog I had at the time, when I lost my phone.

Since then I have always made sure to save my photos to my computer, as well as saving the best ones to an external hard drive.

I have my phone set up now so as any photos I take are immediately uploaded to Microsoft one drive.

For those that don't know, one drive is a storage service that saves your photos or documents on one of Microsoft's servers. A similar service is available from Google.

By doing this I've ensured that all my photos are safe. I print out the ones I really like and have them printed out in my local superstore for a really low price. I then put them in real photo albums – just like the old days!

I have an album specifically for photos of the dogs I have owned and that album is my way of memorialising each and every dog I have owned.

I also have lots of videos of my last dog that I've saved to discs and on my computer which I view from time to time.

Photos and videos are the simplest way of memorialising your dog but below is a list of other methods that many people use, and one may stand out for you.

Commission a painting

As mentioned above, my friend has an oil painting of his dog hanging proudly in his home. He takes great comfort in looking at it and prefers it to a photograph.

The cost of commissioning a painting can be very high and there are far cheaper options such as having a photograph transferred onto a canvas.

It's possible these days to send a photo via the internet to a company who will transfer it to canvas for you and mail you the product.

However, if you really do want a painting, make sure you see examples of the artist's work before you commission him or her and ensure you use a great photograph as reference material.

Have a detailed conversation with the artist about your dog and his or her personality – you want a true likeness of your dog to shine through in the completed painting.

Never be afraid to ask for updates on the painting and even ask to view it as it progresses.

As somebody who used to paint, I would also suggest that you consider having a painting done in acrylic paint rather than oil. Acrylic paint has a very fast drying time and is far more forgiving when it comes to correcting mistakes.

Acrylic paint will not yellow or crack over time either, as oil paint does, and the finished products are very hard to tell apart.

Many modern artists have made the change from oil to acrylic so you will find plenty of talented people to carry out the work for you.

Erect a simple plaque

If you have chosen not to bury your dog and have a headstone, you could still choose to have a simple plaque made, with a picture of the dog engraved on it, and a little text.

You could place it in your dog's favourite spot in the garden or even have an indoor one made that can be framed.

Tattoos

Many people choose to permanently memorialise their dog on their skin in the form of a tattoo.

It doesn't have to be large and can be a portrait of the dog or just the dog's name.

It's even possible to find tattooists that will mix some of your dog's ashes with the ink used for the tattoo.

This option isn't for everybody but some people do find great comfort in it.

Jewellery

This is a great option to consider.

There are companies that will add the ashes or hair of your dog to rings, lockets and other items of jewellery so you can always carry or store safely, a permanent reminder of your dog.

It can be costly depending on the piece you choose, but no more so than a good headstone.

I'm sure that there are lots of other ways to remember your dog and I'm sure you'll do it in your own special way.

However you choose to memorialise your dog, be it just through memories, or as a large painting, the main thing to remember is that the dog is memorialised in your heart permanently.

If you don't wish to have a physical reminder of your dog there's nothing wrong with that – he or she will always live within yours and the hearts of all the people that loved him, and at the end of the day – that's all that matters.

CHAPTER 9

A FINAL WORD

Owning a dog is a wonderful experience. Unfortunately, every wonderful experience must eventually come to an end.

We dog lovers do a great service to dogs of all shapes, sizes and backgrounds. Whether you rescued one from a shelter or had one from a puppy, you did that dog a wonderful favour – you gave him or her a life full of happiness, and if your dog could have spoken, he would have told you the same.

The emotions you are experiencing now will fade in time – you must believe that.

Eventually you will look back on your dog's life with little sadness and great joy, and you will release yourself of all the unfounded guilt you have burdened yourself with. I promise you that.

Thank you for taking the time to read this book and I wish you all the best in progressing through this awful time in your life. You will get through it.

Richard Oliver

Made in United States
North Haven, CT
23 November 2022

27115709R00020